Find Your Passion: 25 Questions You Must Ask Yourself

By
Henri Junttila

Table of Contents

Introduction

Let's face it.

Finding and following your passion is tough.

You've probably read advice that tells you to "just follow your passion," but you know that it isn't that easy. This is a scary, overwhelming and confusing journey.

It's hard to know when, where, and how to start.

And even if you manage to get started, your inner demons pop up. Suddenly you're paralyzed by fear and all you want to do is hide under the bed covers. The good news is that this is normal. Just because you're confused, uncertain and afraid, doesn't mean you have to stop.

In fact, it means that you're on the right path. It means that you're pushing your boundaries and doing something new. The bottom line is that you can live a passionate life. Deep down you already know that. Otherwise you wouldn't be reading this.

You don't have to quit your job.

You don't have to make radical changes in your life.

You just have to take one tiny step at a time.

You see, I believe you already have everything you need inside of you. You are good enough the way you are. You've simply learned ideas that keep you from living up to your full potential.

This book will not only help you find your passion, but also help you uncover the limitations you've created for yourself. This isn't about a quick-fix, but about putting in the work and discovering what's truly stopping you from moving forward.

You don't have to wait to live a passionate life. You can start right here, right now. But you have to be willing to take the next step. Joseph Campbell put it well when he said, "Follow your bliss and the universe will open doors for you where there were only walls."

Find Your Passion

If you're ready to be honest with yourself, and you're ready to take action, then you're in the right place.

Who Am I?

So, what makes me an expert on living a passionate life?

First, I don't consider myself an expert.

I've built a business doing work I love. I've lived an unconventional life ever since I got out of high school. At the tender age of 18, I became a professional online poker player. I played poker for five years, before I realized that something was missing.

In the midst of my poker career, I started playing around with websites. I wasted over $10,000 on get rich quick scams and bad coaching. I spent years trying to figure things out.

In 2009 something clicked, and when it did, things took off.

At the end of 2009, my girlfriend and I (and our dog), moved to Spain for a year, all thanks to my online business.

Ever since that year, I've been making a full-time living online. Each year I've learned more about myself. Each year I'm living life more aligned with my heart. It was at the end of 2009 that I started a blog called Wake Up Cloud. I didn't have any grand plans for it. I simply wanted to share my views on life.

But life has a tendency to surprise us, and that's exactly what happened. People quickly got interested in what I had to say, and I attracted a readership of thousands within just a few months.

People wanted to know how I was able to follow my passion, live in Spain, and overcome my fears. That's where all this started. I'm not an expert, but I do know a thing or two about what works and what doesn't.

Today, we're no longer living in Spain. We've returned back to Finland, where our family is. We also became parents in late 2011 to an amazing baby boy.

The work I do allows me to spend a large chunk of my day with my son and the people I care about. And it makes my heart sing to follow my passion. So you see, I'm here to share with you what I've found to work in my life, and in the lives of the people I've helped.

With this book, I hope I can help you, too.

Free Gift

There's a free gift available just for the buyers of this book. It's a PDF workbook with all the questions, and all the prompts, so you can print it out and know exactly where you left off.

I've also added a few bonus questions to the workbook. You'll find the link to your free gift at the end of this book.

How to Use This Book

This book is divided into sections. Each of those sections focuses on just one of the passion questions.

There is no right or wrong way to answer these questions. The only mistake you can make is to not answer them.

These questions are springboards into the depth of your mind, heart and spirit. Because you already have the answers you're seeking. You already know what you need to know. You only have to uncover what's already there.

As you dive into the first few questions, you'll immediately notice that this is not just about discovering your passion. It's also about uncovering how you hold yourself back. Some of these questions you may have heard before, but that doesn't make them ineffective. My goal here is not to wow you with "new" questions, but to help you move forward.

It's scary to jump into the unknown. That's why many people would rather keep attending seminars, reading books, and pretending to make changes. Ultimately it's up to you to take responsibility for your life.

The questions in this book will help you see what's stopping you, what you're passionate about, and what next steps you need to take. The only thing you need to get the most out of this book is a pen and a notebook (or a piece of paper).

If you want to explore the questions on your computer, that's fine, but I recommend good old pen and paper. It's a touch more magical that way. Here's how I recommend you go through each section:

1. Read the whole section.

2. Use the Time to Write sub-section to keep you on track.

3. Write down whatever comes to mind as you dive into the questions and prompts.

In short, all you have to do is read each section and then explore the question via writing. If you've never done this before, don't worry, simply write down what you're thinking. You don't have to be a writer. And you can't do this wrong.

A Note on Overwhelm

This book is meant to be taken in slowly. The more time you spend with each question, the more clarity you will get.

When you put in the work, I guarantee that you will gain insight into how you can start moving toward living the life of your dreams. You'll discover what's stopping you, and you'll discover what makes your heart sing.

But before you get there, you'll probably feel uncomfortable, confused and uncertain. That's normal. Sometimes this takes time. Let it be okay, and let life happen. You don't have to try and figure things out or force progress.

I know you're eager to get started, so let's dive into the first question, shall we?

1. The Definition Trap

Question: How do you define passion?

Have you ever looked at what your definition of passion is? Most people haven't. They're trying to build a passionate life, all while having no idea what it is.

How can you know you've arrived if you don't know what you're after?

This question is about diving into what ideas, beliefs and thoughts you have around the word passion. It's about uncovering unrealistic expectations of what living your passion means.

When you look beyond the label, you'll discover that this isn't about finding your passion.

It's about enjoying this moment.

It's about waking up, feeling excited to be alive, and feeling grateful to be doing what you're doing.

You jump out of bed, humming, and ready to tackle the day. Your life isn't devoid of problems, but you have an inner drive and energy guiding you through life.

You're living life through your heart. You feel fulfilled, because you feel like you're where you need to be. There's meaning to your life. And when you feel like this, you affect everyone around you. You contribute in a meaningful way to the world.

This doesn't happen overnight. And even now, as I'm doing work I love and following my passion, I still face challenges, because that's how this game we call life works.

But the bottom line is that you can start turning up the excitement, enjoyment, and passion in your life, right now.

To do that, you have to look at what passion truly means to you. You have to look at what the word is pointing to.

Possible Roadblocks

You may not feel entirely comfortable exploring this question. In fact, you may not feel comfortable with most of the questions in this book.

But discomfort is a good sign. If you notice discomfort, you've reached the core of the issue. The goal of this question is to uncover any false ideas you have surrounding the word passion.

As you do this, you will have to go through what your friends, family and society has told you that passion is, and you have to uncover what it means for you, because that's the only thing that matters.

Time to Write

Start by answering the question: "How do I define passion?" Look at what you believe passion is. What ideas, thoughts and beliefs do you have around it?

Grab your pen and paper, and start writing without censoring yourself. Let whatever comes out, come out. Dump your mind on paper.

If you run out of things to say, just write whatever comes to mind, such as "I don't know what to say. This is weird. I'd like some chocolate ice cream."

Keep writing through good feelings and bad feelings. If you go off track, gently bring yourself to the original question.

And if you need extra help, each section in this book has prompts that will get you going. Simply read the prompts and complete them. Here's what they look like for this section:

- Passion for me means …
- Passion for my friends and family means …
- When I'm living a passionate life, it looks …
- When I'm following my passion, I feel …

Living a passionate life is rarely what you think it is. You've picked up ideas, concepts and thoughts about what life should be. When you realize this and readjust your expectations, your life will change for the better.

2. End Goal

Question: How will you know when you're living a passionate life?

Once you know what your definition of passion is, it's time to look at what your end goal is.

It's crucial that you uncover how you'll know that you're living a passionate life. What are the signs that will tell you that you've arrived?

It's rarely money, wealth, fame or any of those things. It's something beyond that.

When I did this, I had several a-ha moments. When I started looking at what passion meant for me, it came down to enjoying this moment, just like I mentioned earlier.

In the past, I believed money was the answer to everything. That belief was shattered when I was a professional poker player. I had enough money to travel the world and do what I wanted, yet I still felt like something was missing.

That's because happiness, joy and passion come from the inside.

As I began looking at what living a passionate life meant, I discovered that what I truly cherished were experiences, relationships and being able to express my heart.

I wanted to be happy right here, right now. That's when something shifted. I asked myself "Well, what's stopping me from being happy right now?"

And the answer?

Ideas.

Ideas, beliefs, and thoughts I'd picked up throughout the years.

Following your passion doesn't have to be a thing in the future. Yes, you may not be where you want to be. You may have goals, which is fine.

But you don't have to agonize over not being somewhere. You will always be evolving and growing. That isn't the issue. The issue is how you relate to life.

Possible Roadblocks

Beware of your own assumptions when you explore this question. Look at what you believe to be true.

Also beware of vagueness. Be willing to dive into the specifics of how you will know when you're living a passionate life. This will start showing you if you're on a wild goose chase or if you're actually being realistic.

For example, for me the signs that I was making progress were increased inspiration and happiness. My heart was bursting with excitement. My life started flowing more smoothly. Not without challenges, but I felt better.

You may discover that you have unrealistic expectations of what a passionate life is. You may discover that you're not after passion at all, but after the approval of others.

This may be scary, but consider this: when you move through the discomfort, your mind will open up to a world of new possibilities. And this is what you're after, isn't it?

Time to Write

Once again, start with the question, "How will I know when I'm living a passionate life?"

Then use the prompts below to help you get going and to look at this from different angles.

Write completely uncensored. If you veer off track, bring yourself back to the question above or one of the prompts below. Let go of trying to find a specific answer and just write. Play with it.

- When I find my passion, my life will be …
- When I find my passion, I will feel …
- I will know I've found my passion when …

Our definitions define us, so make sure you go through these first few questions. If you don't know what you're after, or where you're going, chances are that you won't end up where you want to be.

When you're ready, the next question will be waiting for you.

3. Dreams Come True

Question: What will you do when you've found your passion?

In the last question we looked at how you will know you're living a passionate life. Let's look at what you will do once you've arrived at your "final" destination.

Once you're living a passionate life and everything is perfect, what then? What will you do? How will you behave?

A trap I've fallen into countless times is thinking that I need something before I can be happy. For example, I'm a pretty quiet guy.

But when life is going my way, I'm more outgoing, light-hearted and fun to be around. On the flip side, when life isn't doing what I want it to, I become even more introverted.

So what's going on is that I have a formula for being miserable. If X happens, I can be Y. But what if I were to flip that formula around? What if I were Y (happy) even if X didn't happen?

That's what this question is all about.

We're all waiting for something, so what are you waiting for?

What's stopping you from doing what you want to do?

And what's stopping you from being happy, right now?

This question may seem strange to ask in a book about finding your passion, but it's important that you explore it.

Remember that the word passion is just a label. It's a word, and like all words, it points to something beyond it, like a signpost pointing to a city. It's easy to forget this and believe that the signpost is the city.

Possible Roadblocks

Notice any thoughts coming up to dismiss this question, or any question in this book. We're laying the groundwork here for later questions.

Ask your mind if it would be willing to experiment with this question just for a few minutes. Set all your worries, anxieties and fears aside while you write.

You can have them back later.

When you write down what you would do (and how you would behave) once you've found your passion, you can start behaving that way right now. It's not easy, but you can start.

Time to Write

Start by answering the question: "What will I do when I've found my passion?"

Write for 5-10 minutes. If you don't have anything to say, just write whatever comes up, even if it seems random.

Then dive into the writing prompts below.

- When I find my passion, I will finally …
- When I'm living the life of my dreams, I will …
- I haven't found my passion yet, so it's okay for me to …
- For me it's important to find my passion, because …

Is your brain starting to feel overloaded yet? If it is, it's a sign that you're changing.

This is a lot like going to the gym. Right after, your muscles will hurt, but within a few days, your muscles will have grown stronger, faster and better.

16

4. Mindset

Question: What would you have to believe about yourself to live a passionate life?

What's one belief you have about yourself that keeps you from finding and following your passion?

For a long time, I didn't think I could draw. When I was 6 years old, I remember sitting at my desk, trying to draw something, and it was never as good as real drawings. I crumpled up the paper, threw my pencils on the floor and gave up.

I wanted to scream. I wasn't good enough. I couldn't draw. I didn't want to even try to draw. And I didn't for another 20 years. I've been avoiding drawing for all this time, because I didn't BELIEVE I could do it.

But in June 2012, I joined a cartooning course. I started practicing drawing on a daily basis. At first, it was frustrating, because I was coming up against my beliefs.

One day I had the sudden realization that I could draw. My belief had shifted. I started posting my cartoons publicly, and people were inspired by what I did.

This made me think, "If I believed that I couldn't draw, and now I can, what else is possible?"

Beliefs seem real, because that's their job. If your beliefs fell apart at the drop of a hat, your life would be a mess. The job of your beliefs is to seem immovable.

So what would you have to believe in order to find and follow your passion?

Do you think you're not worthy of doing something you enjoy? Maybe you think you have nothing to share with the world. Maybe you think you don't have enough time.

Whatever it may be, notice that these are merely ideas that you have.

I'm not saying this to put you down. I'm saying it to help you take a step back, and look at your life from a different perspective.

This isn't about life accommodating you, this is about you making the decision to start. It's about becoming ruthless about what you want.

Possible Roadblocks

As you explore this question, look out for ideas that try to stop you from living a passionate life.

For example, you may think that you have to quit your job in order to follow your passion. That's an idea that is holding you back, because you don't have to do anything radical.

You just have to be willing to start. And you can start even if you have just 10 minutes a day to spare. There's no need to wait for anything.

Time to Write

Just for a moment, forget about finding your passion. Start by asking yourself, "What would I have to believe to live a passionate life?"

What ideas would you have to hold as true to follow your heart?

This question will show you what's holding you back. And as you know, most of the time, you're the only one holding yourself back.

Here are a few writing prompts to help you get going:

- To stay where I am, I would have to believe ...

- In order to make my passion happen, I would have to believe ...

- If I believed that (see above prompt), my next step would be ...

We're making progress, aren't we?

Don't worry if you don't have immediate clarity. It may take days or even weeks, but it will come. Let your brain chew on this.

While you wait, remember to relax and enjoy the ride.

5. The Teacher in You

Question: What do other people ask you about?

Before I started helping people live a passionate life and build a business around something they love, I seemed to naturally get questions about mindset, life, and things related to personal development.

People would come to me with all kinds of ideas and ask me what I thought.

But I didn't believe I could just start sharing my tips online. I mean, who was I to give advice when there were so many established "experts" already out there?

This held me back for several years, until I'd had enough. I snapped. Suddenly I didn't care if I failed. I didn't care about my fears. I was ready to challenge my assumptions and ideas.

I wanted to at least see what would happen. And you know what happened?

People started reading what I had to say. My blog grew to thousands of readers within a few short months. Yes, I had to put in a lot of work. But it showed me that once again, I had held myself back from doing something that made my heart sing.

This question is simple. You may come up with answers that you think aren't feasible. Maybe your friends ask you about what perfume to wear when they go out, or where to eat on a first date.

Don't dismiss anything. Follow the thread, and explore.

Possible Roadblocks

When you play with this question, be aware of any thoughts coming up that negate your findings. For example, if you've always wanted to be a writer, but you don't think you can write, that's what I'm referring to.

The reason I keep pointing to the same roadblock is because this is what I see holding people back over and over again.

If fears come up, or if thoughts of "I can't" come up, just keep writing and exploring. If you want to, you can write down your fears on a separate piece of paper to satisfy them.

Time to Write

Begin by exploring the question: "What do people come to me for advice about?"

Once you've done that. Dive into the prompts below. Remember to write freely. Write uncensored, and keep writing even if you run out of things to write.

- When people ask me for advice, they generally ask about …

- I really enjoy helping people with …

- I hate helping people with …

- I feel fulfilled when I help people …

The most obvious things are the things we miss. And the things we miss are the things that make us come alive.

6. Personality Discovery

Question: What's your personality?

Something I've found immensely helpful in uncovering my passion is to look at what I'm naturally good at.

There are several personality tests out there that are quite good at this. One that I and the people I've helped have found particularly helpful is the Myers-Briggs personality test.

I also like the Enneagram, which goes into a lot of depth on your strengths and weaknesses.

If you go to a search engine and type in "myers-briggs personality test," you'll find a few free ones that will get you started.

As for the Enneagram, I recommend you go to the Enneagram Institute at enneagraminstitute.com. Remember, these tests are not meant to give you an exact answer. They're meant to act as springboards, much like this book.

Before you go and do any of those tests, focus on this section. Explore the questions here. When you're done, you can compare your writing to the results you get from the personality tests above.

Possible Roadblocks

We tend to dismiss what comes naturally and easily to us. For example, I find writing easy. I'm a natural problem solver and I have the ability to be very practical.

These are things that come so easily to me that for a long time I thought I couldn't possibly create a business around them.

Eventually, I came to my senses. I realized that when I was working with my strengths, I was happy and energized, even if I ran into challenges. We'll dive deeper into your strengths in the next question.

Time to Write

Start with the question: "What's my personality?" I've made this question vague on purpose. I want you to riff on it and see what comes out.

If you go into negative territory at first, let it be okay. Bring yourself back to the positive aspects of your personality. Once you're done exploring, try the prompts below.

- I absolutely hate doing …
- People tell me what I have natural knack for …
- My personality lends itself to …

We have all these ideas of what we can and can't do. We often grow up with family, friends and society telling us what's possible. We learn to suppress our natural passions.

It's not easy to uncover them, but you've already begun the process. Let any fear, confusion and overwhelm be okay. Remember that it's okay to take a break. This isn't about getting results right this very minute.

This is about exploration.

7. Strengths

Question: What comes easy to you?

We looked at your personality in the last question. Now let's look at your strengths.

When you tap into your strengths, you'll experience increased happiness and decreased depression in your life. I'm not just making this up. There's a lot of research behind this.

It doesn't matter if you're stuck in a job you don't like, because when you start using more of your strengths, you'll become happier, and yes, more passionate about life.

So how do you figure out what your strengths are?

Start by looking at what activities make your heart sing. What gives you a sense of freedom and excitement when you do them?

For example, for me it's writing. I love writing. It's not always easy, but more often than not, I feel a sense of freedom, flow and excitement when I'm writing.

Once you have a list of activities you enjoy, look at what strengths you're using in each. For me in writing, it would be:

- Honesty
- Simplicity
- Perspective
- Creativity

I could go deeper, but I think you get the gist of it.

Once I have this list, I can explore how I could use these signature strengths in other areas of my life. Just thinking about it makes my heart buzz with excitement.

If I wanted to, I could dive even deeper into my strengths list and explore what it looks like when I use honesty in my writing, for example. That would give me a better idea of how to apply it in other parts of my life.

So you see, you don't have to "find" your passion, because you can start turning up the amount of passion in your life right away.

Tap into your strengths and watch the passion in your life soar.

Possible Roadblocks

The roadblock you should be aware of is confusion.

If you're like me, you may feel like you need a list of strengths to choose from. But for now, pretend that you have that list, and pick whatever comes to mind.

Remember, you are the only person who knows what's going on inside you. You can make up your own words and categories, because words point to something beyond them.

The words are not as important as the feeling behind the word.

Time to Write

Let's discover your strengths.

Start by exploring the question, "What comes easy to me?"

And then dive into the prompts:
- When I'm working at my best, I am …
- What I find easy, and what makes my heart sing, is …
- If I pretended to know, I'd say I was good at …

Feel free to expand on these questions. Don't just answer with one or two words. Push yourself to write at least one paragraph or more.

The more you write, the more insight you will get.

8. Humble Beginnings

Question: What are (or were) your interests?

I'm sure you've explored your interests before, but I recommend you do it again. And this time I suggest you do it without censoring yourself. Just write whatever comes to mind.

Why?

Because more often than not, your passion is hiding in plain sight.

The problem is that life tends to get in the way of your interests. Challenges come up and suddenly you don't have time for "fun" anymore.

You focus on making ends meet, or following the advice of your peers, and it slowly devours you from the inside. After a while, you start feeling miserable, because you've gone off track.

This question is about reconnecting to the interests you had in the past, or have right now.

Let's take an example you're already familiar with—my writing. I still remember coming up with crazy stories when I was seven years old. People loved the quirkiness of them.

But as the years passed, I forgot about my love for writing. Luckily, I rediscovered it, and here I am, writing this book.

The key is to not dismiss anything that comes up. Go through all the interests that have made an appearance in your life. Then look at which ones you resonate with today.

Possible Roadblocks

Watch out for not taking this question seriously. It may seem simple, but as you dive deeper, you'll uncover gold. The key is to keep writing when you run out of things to write.

Remember, you only have to find one clue that you can follow. This isn't about coming up with your passion right here on the spot. It's about realizing that things take time.

And that you only have to move forward one tiny step at a time. Don't worry about where this will lead. Just focus on this moment and this question.

Time to Write

Start by exploring the question, "What are, or were, my interests?"

Write down anything and everything that comes to mind.

And when you're ready, dive into the prompts below:

- When I was younger, I wanted to become …
- When I was a child, I always loved doing …
- Right now, I'm fascinated by …
- I love learning about …
- The reason is because …

Remember to take breaks. Don't try to do all of these questions at once. Although if you're anything like me, you'll do it anyway.

9. True Desires

Question: What do you REALLY want?

By really, I mean truly, deep in your heart.

We grow up and we're told that our dreams are impossible. We're told that we should settle for what's practical.

But what we don't realize as children is that those words are not coming from an authority. They come from a person who has been defeated. They come from people who unconsciously keep others down to feel better about themselves. We listen, and we hide away the passions that truly move us.

More often than not they come from friends and family. There's nothing wrong with this. I love my family. I love my friends. But we have to get to the core of the issue if we want to move forward. What would you want if no one had ever told you no?

Pretend that you step into a time machine. You take a trip back to the past where you shared your dreams with someone and they turned you down. Or when a similar event happened where you thought that you couldn't go after what you truly wanted.

What was that thing? What was it that you wanted?

It doesn't have to be your passion, but it can give you an idea. It can be a springboard to something else. Are you noticing how much emphasis I put on the fact that this is about exploration? Could you begin to explore what you really want?

Let go of wanting to get the answer, and let the answer come to you. It may not come in the form you expect. This question is all about letting go of your assumptions, of the ideas you've learned, and the thoughts that hold you back.

Let them go for just a second and see what you discover.

Possible Roadblocks

Look out for thoughts that come up that try to hold you back. They'll tell you that you can't do this, this isn't possible, and that you might as well give up. They will tell you it is not safe to know what you really want. These are not your thoughts, but thoughts you've picked up from others.

You didn't come into this world with these thoughts. They are not yours. Let them go.

In this book, you'll notice that I repeat a few core messages from different angles. This is by design. The more you are exposed to these ideas, the more your life will change.

It may not happen all at once, but in the days and months to come, interesting things will happen. But you have to be willing to put in the work with these questions.

Time to Write

As always, start with the main question: "What do I really want?"

Then go deeper with the prompts below.

- When I was younger, I always wanted to ...
- What I want, but secretly believe I can never have/do/be, is ...
- The reason I want that is because ...
- The way I want to contribute to the world is by ...
- If no one had told me no, I would've wanted ...

29

Find Your Passion

That's that for this question. If you need a break, take it. You've earned it. When you're ready, I'll be waiting for you on the next page.

10. Please No!

Question: What don't you want?

We just looked at what you want. Now it's time to look at what you DON'T want.

When you ask this question, don't settle for a superficial answer. If you do, you might just end up with "I don't want to work for someone else, and I don't want to be unhappy."

Those are great starting points, but you have to push yourself. Ask yourself why you don't want to do those things. Dive into the details.

Let's take an example from my life...

I don't want to work in a job that hampers my natural curiosity. I want to be free to express myself and to grow. Why? I want to be able to inspire others and help change the world.

Why?

Because I feel like people can do more, be more, and live more. I may not be perfect, but I want to share the inspiration I feel inside of me.

How?

I want to write, speak, or do whatever it takes to get the message out. I want to express what's inside my heart.

How can I start doing this?

I can start by inspiring just one person. I can start a blog. I can write a short essay. I can share quotes. I can be happier around my friends. I can just be who I am.

Are you seeing where I'm going with this?

I'm constantly going deeper by asking why and how. I start by exploring what I don't want, and then I let it lead me to what I do want.

31

Possible Roadblocks

It seems I got a bit fired up and covered most of the roadblocks you'll face with this question.

It's crucial that you keep diving deeper into this question. Keep asking why and how. When you ask the right questions, the right answers almost come out by themselves.

Don't be too hard on yourself if you don't get this right away. It takes practice to get good at going deeper. And you have to let yourself be crappy before you get good.

You're already doing your best. Let that be okay. You don't have to be someone you're not. All you have to do is what you are able to do. Sounds almost too simplistic, doesn't it?

Time to Write

The only thing you have to remember is to keep going deeper. Dive into the details. Don't settle for easy, superficial answers.

As always, start with the main question, "What don't I want?"

And when you're ready, use these friendly prompts:
- The most horrible version of my life is …
- I really hate …
- I hate seeing people …

Keep diving deeper. Go into more and more detail. Even when you run out of things to say, keep asking yourself why and how.

You can always go deeper.

11. Quitting

Question: What would happen if you gave up right now?

Let's explore what your life would look like if you didn't follow your passion.

I've been doing work I love since 2009. Each year I've gone deeper, and I've discovered that I can enjoy life even more. But each year I've also come up against challenges that have made me want to throw in the towel.

I've had to rethink the way I do business several times. I've had to push my boundaries. And each time, I've wanted to give up. I've felt overwhelmed. But eventually, I've gotten through it.

And as the years have passed, I've gotten better at handling challenges. I've become more gentle with myself. I don't try to force progress as much. When I feel frustrated, I do my best to take a break and let my unconscious chew on the problem.

I let my heart guide me in the right direction. And more often than not, I get the answer I need. When I don't, I move forward and do my best.

But what I can never seem to do is give up. I know where giving up leads. It would give me temporary relief. However, I know that after that relief, there would be regret.

My heart keeps telling me to keep going. My mind is screaming. My fears are coming up. But my heart is steady. It's the subtle whisper behind all the noise.

And the same is true for you. We're all built the same way. It doesn't matter if you believe in this or not. If you look inside, you'll discover an inner GPS. It might

33

be a voice, a feeling, a picture, or a green elf waiting to help you when you most want to give up.

Most people have neglected their inner GPS. They've stopped trusting themselves. To reconnect with it, you have to make a decision to listen.

Possible Roadblocks

Exploring this question is uncomfortable, because it will show you where you are headed if you settle for a comfortable life.

Now, if you've just started changing how you live, you have nothing to worry about. Come to think of it, the fact that you're reading this book shows that you're following your heart. It shows that you're ready to take things to the next level.

You may feel like giving up at times, but know that you're on the right path, and you are good enough. I just wanted to throw this in here. Don't take things so seriously. Let life take care of itself, you just enjoy the ride.

Time to Write

As human beings, we're wired to go for the quick fix. We're wired for instant satisfaction. The questions in this section will help you see what the results of those actions are.

Most people live their life following their wiring and it leads to regret. These questions may not be pleasant, but they will be revealing.

Start by exploring the main question, "What would happen if I gave up?"

Then dive into the prompts:

- If I stopped following my heart, in 5 years my life would be …

- In 10 years, my life would …
- If I took tiny steps, even though I might struggle, in 5 years I would …
- In 10 years of following my heart, my life would …

Interesting, isn't it?

12. Inner Voice

Question: What is your inner voice whispering?

In the last chapter, we touched on that subtle voice we all have inside of us. Or if you prefer, your inner GPS. It doesn't matter what you call it, it's still there, waiting for you to listen.

Most of us are too busy to pay attention to our inner GPS. We're so focused on getting things done that we forget to relax.

We forget to take breaks.

I fall into the same pattern. When I go for a long stretch without consulting my GPS, I start to lose my bearing.

I see my inner voice as my GPS, so if I don't consult it from time to time, I don't know where I'm going. The way I listen to my inner voice is through meditation. But I also get bursts of inspiration while walking, cleaning, playing with my son, or just living life. The secret is to become quiet enough to hear that inner whisper. And meditation helps you do that.

You don't have to sit down on a pillow to meditate. All you have to do is become aware of your thoughts right now. You don't even have to try and quiet your mind.

You just have to observe. Close your eyes and imagine that your thoughts are on a TV screen in front of you. Just watch them float by. Don't touch any thoughts. Remain as the observer of the TV.

Sooner or later, a thought will pull you in, just like a good movie does from time to time. It will seem important. This is to be expected. When you notice that you've been pulled in, simply return to observing your mind.

Meditating just a few minutes each day will make a big difference. There are a lot of studies out there showing how meditation can change your brain, and your life, for the better. And as you practice quieting your mind, you will hear your inner voice more often.

A great resource for easily incorporating meditation into your life is Headspace. You can find it at http://www.getsomeheadspace.com/.

Now, you can also consult your inner voice via writing, which is what we're going to do in this section.

Possible Roadblocks

The only mistake you can make is to not do this exercise. I've found that I get the best results when I use regular pen and paper. That is, not writing on my computer.

Although if I ever get stuck on something, I'll write on my computer and coach myself, but we'll talk about that later in this book.

Whatever comes up as you do this exercise, keep writing. Dump your mind on paper. Take the burden off of your mind and give it to the paper in front of you. The more you do this, the clearer your mind will become, and the more access you will have to your inner GPS.

Keep coming back to the question: "What does my inner voice want me to know, right now?"

Time to Write

Start with the main question, "What is my inner voice whispering?"

At first, you may not hear anything. Or you may not hear what you want to hear. This is normal. Just pretend that you're hearing something.

When you're ready, use these prompts to take you further:

- In order to connect with my inner voice, I have to …

- If I had a source of inner wisdom inside me, it would say …

- My heart really yearns to …

How did it go?

You did the exercise, didn't you? If not, put down this book and do it right now. If you don't have 15 minutes, do it for just a minute.

Whatever you do, don't move on until you've done this. You owe it to yourself.

13. Make-Believe

Question: If you pretended to know, what would your passion be?

Remember back to your childhood, when you spent hours daydreaming and pretending.

You pretended to be in a world far, far away. But somewhere along the line, you stopped. It's time to start up again. Because when you pretend to know something, or when you allow yourself to daydream, your brain activates your problem solving powers.

A 2009 University of British Columbia study discovered that when you daydream, certain regions in your brain are activated which increase creative problem solving.

In the study, the researchers found that when people are involved in simple tasks, where their minds daydream, these "problem solving" regions in their brain light up like lighthouses.

This is why sometimes when you're in the shower, reading a book, or doing the dishes, you suddenly have a burst of insight.

But this burst of insight doesn't happen unless you've thought about a problem. This is where the questions in this book come in.

When you explore these questions in-depth, you may not come up with answers right away, but when you step back, your brain goes to work on them.

This is also why I recommend you take breaks. It helps to put the book down in-between questions and let your mind wander. It helps your brain consolidate what you've learned.

Now, the beauty of this question is that you can use it in conjunction with any other question in this book. For example, if I'm stuck on a project or problem, I'll just ask myself, "If I pretended to know the answer, what would it be?"

Or I might focus on my next step and ask, "If I pretended to know the next step, what would it be?"

When you allow yourself to imagine what could be, it will allow your mind to see new possibilities.

Possible Roadblocks

This question may seem like a cheap trick, but it's far from it. Life isn't about struggling to get answers. It's about asking questions and letting the answer come to you. An easy way to do this is to pretend.

Answers rarely come in the way you expect. So be open and see what bubbles up. This definitely isn't easy. I want to force progress like anyone else. But I've noticed that I just end up feeling frustrated and exhausted if I try to control everything.

We have to remember that we're human, and we have our limitations. But we also have to remember that we have a lot of untapped potential.

Time to Write

Let's dive into the writing.

Begin by exploring the main question, "If I pretended to know, what would my passion be?"

And once you've done that for 5-15 minutes, feel free to move to the prompts below:

- If I pretended to know, I would want to …
- If I was connected to my inner wisdom, it would tell me to …
- If I let myself daydream, I …

Let your imagination run wild with this one.
And remember to take a break and daydream. There's no rush.

14. The Impossible

Question: What would you do if you knew you couldn't fail?

Fear of failure can paralyze the best of us. Many of my readers, customers and clients believe that I have somehow overcome the fear of failure. But I haven't.

Failure looms in the back of my mind. Sometimes stronger, sometimes weaker. I don't see it as an enemy, but an ally.

It makes sure that I don't rush into decisions. Yes, it may sometimes cause stabbing anxiety, but that's a part of being human.

We experience the full spectrum of emotions. The problems begin when you try to not feel something. When you feel the fear of failure fully, it abates. Sounds counter-intuitive, doesn't it? Try it out next time you experience a strong emotion. It works.

This question will help you connect to your heart and see where it wants to go. When you're paralyzed by the fear of failure, it's hard to think straight. You react to the disaster scenarios in your head, which only leads to more anxiety.

Look at it like planting a seed. If the soil is poisoned, nothing will grow. Worst case, you'll end up poisoned.

The same is true for the fear of failure. If you come up with a solution while the soil (your feelings and thoughts) is negative, it will only lead to more negativity.

The solution then is to wait until you feel better, or to use this question to help your mind let go of the fear even if it is for just a minute.

Possible Roadblocks

The pull away from failure can be so strong that it causes you to fail by default. This can happen with bigger aspirations, such as finding your passion, or smaller goals, like answering this question.

Be aware of this tendency while you explore this question. Allow yourself to imagine what you would do if you knew you couldn't fail.

And remember to bring it back to the here and now. Look at what you would do RIGHT NOW if you knew you couldn't fail. What is the next tiny step you would take? The harder this is for you, the bigger the rewards will be.

Time to Write

This is a powerful question. I know you've probably seen it before, but have you explored it in depth? Most people haven't.

I know I certainly didn't for many years. I read self-help books, but I never did the exercises. And I never got the results I wanted.

It wasn't until I started implementing that my life started changing. So start right now. And start by answering the main question, "What would I do if I knew I couldn't fail?"

Then move onto the prompts:

- If I wasn't afraid, I would ...
- If I knew I couldn't fail, the next tiny step I would take would be ...
- If I pretended to have all the confidence and skill I needed, I would ...

Play around with these questions. Feel free to explore and think outside the box. This is your life.

Find Your Passion

These are your answers. You are in charge here. No one else.

15. Guarantees

Question: If you were guaranteed success, what would you do?

The last question was all about failure. Let's look at the flip side and see what would happen if you were guaranteed success. This question may seem similar to the last one, but we're going to approach it from a slightly different angle.

Now, there are no guarantees in the real world, but let's pretend that a magical cat descended from the sky and granted you guaranteed success in one pursuit.

And if you don't like cats, feel free to choose another animal. So, what would you pick? Tap into the freeing power of being guaranteed success. You no longer have to worry about anything other than following what resonates with you.

What would you do?
Where would you go?
How would you think?

Being guaranteed success would allow you to focus on doing what you're interested in while being fully confident that you would get what you want.

No worrying needed. No trying to figure things out. Just focus on what makes your heart sing.

Possible Roadblocks

A common roadblock is that there may not be any one thing you'd want to do. You may have a lot of interests and passions.

If so, write them all down and explore them. Play out their story and where they would lead. Your goal right now is not to try and figure out what path to take, but to explore what resonates with you.

And like I mentioned above, there are no guarantees, but that doesn't mean we can't use this question to uncover hidden treasures.

With any of these questions, the biggest roadblock will be your thoughts, and the ideas you've picked up. Stay focused on exploring what it would be like if you were guaranteed success.

Keep bringing your mind to this question over and over again.

Time to Write

By now, you know how this works, don't you? Begin with the main question, "If I were guaranteed success, what would I do?"

Then dive into the prompts. Notice that these prompts seem similar on the surface to previous ones, but they will take you in different directions the farther you take them. So start with one, and keep exploring.

- If a magic cat descended from the sky and I was guaranteed success, I would ...

- If I could pop a magic pill and be free of limitations, I would ...

- In a perfect world, the next step I would take would be ...

Phew. You've come a long way. If you haven't taken a break, please do. These questions will leave you feeling overwhelmed if you try to do too many at once.

Take a five minute daydreaming break, and I'll see you on the next page when you feel ready.

16. Time Travel

Question: In the future, when you're already living a passionate life, what advice would you give to the present you?

This question is like candy to me.

It just shows you that there are no limits to our imagination. So imagine that you once again step into a time machine and on the other side, you meet the future you, who's already living a passionate life.

This may seem confusing at first, but stick with it. It'll be worth it.

Now ask that future you to tell you what you need to hear right now. What are the next steps you need to take?

Don't worry if you believe you can't visualize. We all visualize in different ways. Let me demonstrate: right now, think about a pink elephant.

Whatever way that pink elephant shows up inside your head is fine. For some it'll be in technicolor, others will feel it, and yet others will hear it. Do it in the way that comes naturally to you.

If you can daydream, you can do this exercise. And if all else fails, you can do it through writing.

Possible Roadblocks

This question requires you to stretch your mind. Be very cognizant of any thoughts that try to stop you. Maybe you believe that you can't visualize. Maybe you think that this question doesn't make sense.

If you truly don't want to do this, then don't. But if you can pretend that you can do it anyway, this question alone will be worth the price of this book.

You see, there is already a version of you living the life you want. You can tap into that wisdom, and you can bring it back to the here and now.

Time to Write

Look at this question as if you were going on an adventure. Imagine yourself traveling to the future and meeting the future you, who is already doing what you want to do.

Then ask yourself: "What helpful advice could this future version of me tell me right now?"

And if you need extra help, here are a few prompts:

- What I really need to hear from my future self is …

- The next step the future version of me would advise me to take would be …

- The one thing future me has realized that I yet haven't is …

Don't you just love the power of your imagination?

If you want, you can have a conversation with that future version of you. Just start writing down questions and answers on a piece of paper and see where it leads.

It may feel like you're making this all up, but so what? As long as it helps, use it to your advantage.

17. Boiling Blood

Question: What makes your blood boil?

When I see people limit themselves, I get angry. I see the potential in people, but they don't do anything about it. They settle for mediocrity, and they believe they can't do better.

Maybe they've picked up a few ideas when they grew up, and now these ideas are holding them back. Now, I'm not perfect. I get stuck just like anyone else. But I'm constantly trying to move forward. I'm not talking about forceful improvement, but simply following my heart.

We all have an inner GPS. If you neglect it, you start feeling lost, unfulfilled and depressed.

So what makes your heart weep?

What would you like to change in the world?

There are a lot of problems to choose from, but there is always one or two that you truly yearn to change.

Where most people get stuck is wanting to create massive change right away, and things don't work that way. Change begins with one step and one person.

It's just like building a house. It begins with laying one brick at a time.

Don't expect things to be amazing all at once. Instead start where you're able to start. You don't have to think big and amazing right away.

Possible Roadblocks

Exploring what makes you angry should be easy. Most people get on a roll when they get to focus on the negative.

What you want to avoid is getting stuck in that negativity. The way you do that is to look at the other side of the coin.

For example, I don't like seeing people hold themselves back. What's the other side of that?

It's asking questions like: How can I change that? What am I able to do? Where can I start? What would I like to see instead?

Time to Write

You probably want to change a lot of things. Start by writing them all down. Then dive deeper into the topics that your heart burns for.

To get started, start with the main question, "What makes my blood boil?"

Then use the prompts below:
- What makes my heart weep is …
- I wish I could change …
- If I think in small steps, I could start by …

A lot of people tell you to think big. That's great, but in order to get going, you have to think small.

When you go and buy groceries, you get there one step at a time. The same is true for contributing to the world and following your heart.

One step is all it takes.

18. Flow

Question: When was the last time you were in a state of flow?

It's easy to forget that you are tapping into your passion all the time. You may not be doing it as often as you'd like, but it helps to realize that you are doing it.

You just have to increase the time you spend there. You do this by looking at when you're in a state of flow, when you feel excited, energized and passionate.

The easy way out on these answers is to explore them superficially. I urge you to go deeper. Keep getting more details and go places you haven't gone before. I know I've been repeating this over and over. That's because it's essential that you put in the work.

For example, I'm in a state of flow right now as I'm writing this. But you may think, "Well that's easy for you to say because you've already found your passion."

But please keep in mind that I didn't always know this. Looking back, I see that I was in flow when I was writing, creating, and helping people. I refused to see it. I don't know why.

Eventually it dawned on me, but it happened little by little. It took me years to uncover what I was good at, and what I was passionate about.

So let it be okay. Let it take the time it takes. It's easy to fall into the trap of wanting to force progress. We all want to move forward faster. But what if you stopped trying so hard? What if you simply focused on increasing the time you spend in a state of effortless flow by 1%?

Possible Roadblocks

You may think that you're never in a state of flow, but you are. There is always a corner of your life where you are already tapping into your passions. You just have to find it.

The things you come up with may feel inconsequential, but don't judge when you explore this question. Focus on writing down whatever comes to your mind.

Also remember to dive into the details. Keep asking why you're in a state of flow when you do a certain thing. What is it about it that you like?

If you start procrastinating or avoiding this question, you know you're on the right track. It's supposed to be uncomfortable.

You've been trying it the easy way. It doesn't work. When you're willing to face the discomfort, everything changes.

Time to Write

I want to once again remind you that there is no right or wrong way to answer these questions.

All you have to concern yourself with is doing the work. As long as you're answering these questions, you're doing fine.

So start by answering the main question, "When was the last time I was in a state of flow?"

And then dive into these prompts:
- The last time I felt energized and free was …
- The reason I'm in a state of flow when I do that is …
- If I pretended to know …
- The one thing I can do to increase the flow in my life is …

See how I slipped in the pretended to know question? Sneaky, huh? It works, and it works well. Go into kid-mode and let yourself daydream.

Let go of your personal feelings around the matter. Let go of the wanting to get things right. Look at it as if you were writing a story—someone else's story.

19. Uncertainty

Question: How does not knowing what you want stop you from taking the next step?

No one has a crystal ball. Certainty doesn't exist. It doesn't need to exist.

The words of author Dan Millman come to mind, "Faith means living with uncertainty—feeling your way through life, letting your heart guide you like a lantern in the dark."

You can't know what your future holds, but you can follow your heart. You can let it guide you through the dark. You may not be used to listening to your heart. You may be used to following your mind and living a "logical" life.

But have you noticed how illogical that logic is? It doesn't lead to happiness.

Uncertainty is a given. At any given point in time, your life can be thrown upside down. Your goal then is not to seek certainty outside of yourself, but to consult your heart. If you've been dismissing your heart, it will take time to reconnect. Allow it to take the time it takes.

The bottom line is that you do not need certainty in order to take the next step. Not knowing is not an obstacle.

This question is about letting go of the need to figure everything out. Because what if you allowed yourself to bask in the uncertainty of life?

What if you allowed life to take care of itself, while you followed your heart? Try it for a day and you'll notice how much lighter you feel.

Possible Roadblocks

You don't have to know what your passion is in order to take the next step. The only thing you have to do is to listen to your heart and see what next step you FEEL like taking.

Sometimes it'll feel like you're walking in a fog. You can only see a few feet ahead of you. If you stand still, nothing happens.

But take just one step forward and you'll see things you didn't see before. This is how life works. When you take the next step, another step will become clear.

So focus on taking one step at a time. The problem is that this may be uncomfortable. But the discomfort is a sign that you're on the right path.

Time to Write

Let's explore this question in more depth, shall we? And remember to have fun. Explore, play, and go crazy. Write upside down. Listen to weird music. Do something you haven't done before. It'll help open up your mind.

The main question is, "How does not knowing what I want stop me from taking the next step?"

When you're done there, you can move to the prompts below:

- If I let go of needing to find my passion, I would …

- If I pretended to know what my next small step was, it would be …

- What I'm truly interested in right now is …

There is no right or wrong way to answer these questions. Whatever makes sense to you is fair game.

20. Hidden Benefits

Question: What are the disadvantages of living a passionate life?

It may seem like there are no disadvantages to getting what you want, but if you're honest with yourself, you will uncover something entirely different.

A simple example of this would be the fact that many people want to be successful, but they're afraid of putting their work out there.

And in most cases, they would have to do exactly what they're afraid of to become successful. Many are not willing to do that, so they hold themselves back from getting what they truly want.

This question is all about exploring the downsides of success. What will happen if you succeed beyond your wildest dreams?

What will your friends, family and peers think? What could go wrong?

What do you think you have to do that you don't want to do?

This will help you uncover some of the hidden blocks that keep you from taking action. So often we sabotage ourselves because we're afraid of what might happen if we succeed.

If you didn't have any apprehensions about living a passionate life, you would already be doing it. There is something holding you back, and you're about to discover what that is.

In my case, I was afraid of failing. I was scared that if I failed, I wouldn't have anything to look forward to. I thought failing would crush my dreams.

Our minds have a tendency to come up with disaster scenarios that seem real. But what happens is that it paralyzes you, and you end up failing without even having tried.

Once I began exploring what was going on, I realized that failure was not possible as long as I was moving forward.

Even if I failed, there was no way for me to know that failing wasn't exactly what needed to happen in order for me to get to my "final destination."

You just can't know what's around the corner. What seems like a disadvantage may turn into an advantage down the road.

Possible Roadblocks

This question can bring out some uncomfortable realizations. You may think that you're ready to follow your passion, but are you really?

There's nothing wrong with admitting the truth. In fact, it's liberating. Once you let go of needing life to look a certain way, you can let it come together all by itself.

You don't have to try and control life. It happens by itself. Stop trying to control everything for a day or two. Instead, let things happen. Let life take care of the seeming disadvantages of outrageous success.

Easier said than done, I know, but do your best.

Time to Write

Are you ready to dive into the benefits of not living the life of your dreams?

Sounds weird when I put it like that, doesn't it? It may sound strange, but once you explore this question, you'll uncover some nuggets.

When you're ready, begin with the main question, "What are the disadvantages of living a passionate life?"

Then, play with the prompts below:

- If I was successful, I would be afraid of …

- The benefits I get from NOT following my passion are …

- If I were to take the next step, I would …

You did use a pen and paper to explore this question, right?

If not, please do it right now. Put this book down and implement. You won't get anywhere by reading. Sure, you may be influenced in a positive way, but if you want real results, you have to be willing to put in the work.

21. Fear

Question: What would you do if you weren't afraid?

This question is similar to #14 where we talked about the fear of failure, so let's approach this question from a different perspective.

Imagine looking through a keyhole. Your vision is limited. Now put the key in the lock, turn it, open the door, and walk through it.

Take a deep breath in and notice how much more you're able to see. You are free from the limitations of the keyhole.

That's what this question does. It helps imagine what your life would be like without some of your fears. So often we get bogged down with fear. We can't see straight. We can't think straight. And we forget to consult our heart.

Your mind will always worry about things. It wants you to be safe. Its job is to be afraid and try to predict what's coming so you can avoid it.

Your fears keep you from living the life you want. So look at what you're afraid of, and ask yourself what you would do if you weren't afraid.

To follow your passion, realize that you don't have to get rid of your fear. You don't have to be fearless. You have to act despite your fear.

This takes courage. And you may not have a lot of courage, which is why it's important to start small. You don't have to quit your job, you just have to do one tiny thing at a time.

And right now, that tiny thing is exploring this question.

59

Possible Roadblocks

What may happen when you ask this question is that you get temporary relief, but then more fears pop up. If that happens, keep asking yourself: "What would I do if even this fear was gone?"

Ask your mind to play along. Eventually you'll gain momentum. Tell your mind that you're running a simulation. You just want to see what it would be like if all your fears were gone for a few minutes.

I use this question often when I am overburdened by fear. It works, if you're willing to dive deep. Yes, I said it again. You have to be willing to dive deep and explore each question.

Time to Write

You can also have a conversation with the part of you that's effective at working with fear.

There are so many possibilities when you open up your imagination. You have all the resources you need to take the next step. It may not feel that way, but that doesn't mean it isn't true.

To get started, ask yourself, "What would I do if I weren't afraid?"

Then dive into the prompts:

- If I could have a conversation with the fearless part of me, it would start with …
- If fear didn't exist, I would …
- The next step I would take if I was fearless would be …

Keep bringing your writing to the present moment. Get it focused on what you can do right now, because that's what matters.

22. Money Matters

Question: What would you do if you had all the money in the world?

You've probably heard this question before. But that doesn't mean it's not powerful. And if you've explored this question previously, you can explore it again.

We tend to seek novelty, but doing new things isn't always a smart idea.

I personally love this question, because it removes barriers from my mind and allows me to open the door instead of looking through the keyhole.

So what would you do if you had all the money in the world? What would you do with that amount of freedom? Once again, the first answers you have may be generic. You might think that you'd travel, sit at home all day or take courses you like.

Make sure you go beyond that. What courses would you take? Where would you travel? What would you do there? Why do you want to do that?

Keep diving deeper into the details. Go beyond the superficial and uncover the underlying motivations. That's when you'll start realizing what your heart truly burns for.

Possible Roadblocks

The first objection you might have is that not thinking about money is delusional. We don't live in an imaginary world. You have to be practical.

Yes, we have to be practical, but you also have to remember that it's impractical to limit yourself in the way you have been.

The purpose of this question is to peek outside the boundaries of what you think is possible. This will help you expand your mind and see new possibilities.

To me, it's impractical to live anything but a passionate life. Yet most people do exactly that. They grow bored with their life, yet they do nothing about it.

Time to Write

There are a few directions you can go. You can go for the up in the clouds answers like changing the world and so on. Or you can focus on the here and now. You could focus on what your heart would want to do right now if money wasn't an issue.

I recommend you do both.

Start by exploring the main question, "What would I do if I had all the money in the world?"

Then dive into the insightful prompts below:

- If I had $100 million in the bank right now, I would ...

- If I had all the money in the world, I would help people with ...

- If I was guaranteed financial security, my small next step would be ...

Most people dream of escaping their life, and they see money as a way to do that. That's why so many people want to become rich.

But you have to remember that money is just a stepping stone to something else. It doesn't remove fear. You still have to take action.

And often, when you follow your passion, you will be both excited and scared, even if you have all the money in the world.

You will still be human.

23. Death

Question: If you had five years left to live, what would you do?

One day, you'll die. After a few years or decades after your death, no one will remember who you were or what you did, unless you changed the world in a big way.

Just you reading this may make you uncomfortable and may make you want to object, but this isn't about who's right. This is about exploring a concept that can help you move forward. So for now, stay open.

Imagining that you'll die may sound depressing, but I find it liberating. It reminds me of the fact that the fears and worries I have are insignificant in the larger scheme of things.

When I look back five years, I can't remember what I worried about. It helps me realize that what I'm worrying about today doesn't matter as much as I think it does. My fears feel real, but they will pass. New fears will take their place, and the cycle will continue.

The reason I want you to imagine you had five years left to live is to give you space. If you imagine you had three months left to live, you would most likely focus on getting your affairs in order.

When we expand the question to five years, your mind will immediately focus on what's important. You'll want to do the things you haven't had time for. You'll want to spend time with your loved ones and you'll want to leap out of your comfort zone.

Possible Roadblocks

When you begin exploring this question, you'll run into things like wanting to spend more time with your family and friends. But once you get past those, that's where the magic happens.

Because what is truly important to you?

Note: I'm not saying family and friends aren't important, but this book is about finding your passion, and that's what we want to uncover.

When you have five years left to live, you have to become focused on what truly matters in your life. Do you want to write that book? Do you want to get up on stage and inspire people?

Do you want to travel the world and tell people about it?

Keep writing and playing out the story of what you would do. Go beyond the obvious and see what comes out.

Time to Write

Imagine that you got your "death sentence" today. You have five years left to live. What would you do? Yes, at first you'd freak out.

But when you get over that, what becomes important? Focus on that, and start writing it down. What is it that your heart would lead you to do?

Here are a few prompts and questions to help you get started:

- If I had five years left to live, I would …
- I would not waste time on …
- What I'm starting to realize is …

And that's that. When you feel eager to move on, I'll be waiting for you on the next page.

24. Problems Poof

Question: If all of your problems were solved, what would you do?

If nothing was stopping you, what next step would you take? Just for a second, could you feel what it would feel like to be free of all your problems, to be free of worry and anxiety?

Feels good, doesn't it?

So often we postpone following our passion. We put off doing what makes our heart sing. Why? Because it seems like we have more important things to do. Or it may seem like you have more urgent problems to solve. These are all excuses. They are not real obstacles. You can start following your passion today.

You don't have to quit your job.

You don't have to fix anything.

You don't have to become someone.

You have to start before you're ready, like Steven Pressfield so eloquently puts it in his book, *Do the Work*.

If you have 5 minutes, which you do, you can start. But where do you start? That's the tough question, isn't it? That's what this book is all about. I'm here to help you take the next step. The problem is that it's easy to make this next step too big. The solution is to think baby steps.

It could be doing some brainstorming, journaling, or signing up for that acting class you've always wanted to take. Forget about where it may lead. If your heart says yes, go for it.

Possible Roadblocks

Once again this comes down to noticing how you've been stopping yourself. Most people will not explore this question. Some may feel uncomfortable with it. That's one of the problems that has been stopping you. What would it be like without it?

Whatever is going on in your head, let it be, and then grab your pen and paper, and start.

Time to Write

Start with the question, "If all my problems were solved, what would I do?"

Explore it for a few minutes, and then dive into the prompts below:

- If I had no problems, worries or challenges, I would …

- If all my excuses suddenly disappeared, I …

- When I imagine being free of my problems, my next (baby) step would be …

All done? How are you feeling? Check in with yourself, take a deep breath and see if you're ready for the next one.

25. Action

Question: How could you take the next step?

It is when you act that the world moves with you. Not before. If you wait for circumstances to be perfect before you act, nothing will happen.

You have to be willing to move forward even if you're uncomfortable. When you're determined to take action no matter what, that's when your life will start falling into place.

We've been talking about taking action. And we've even covered it in a few questions, but it's time to go even deeper.

This question will help you uncover what needs to be in place before you take the next step. It will show you if you're setting yourself up for failure.

As you ask this question, excuses may come up. You may discover that you're a genius when it comes to creating reasons for not taking action. If that happens, keep asking, "How could I take the next step despite this?"

When you ask the right questions, you get the answers you need. Whenever you encounter a roadblock, ask how you could take action anyway.

The sooner you take action, the more progress you'll make. Sounds obvious when I put it like that, doesn't it?

You have to be willing to let go of wanting things to be perfect. You probably won't feel fantastic when you take action. That's fine, and to be expected.

With this question, think in tiny next steps. Instead of having a next step that's "write a book," you'd have "brainstorm book titles I feel excited about," or something even smaller such as "writing in my journal about the apprehension I feel."

Possible Roadblocks

It's all fine and good to consume information. It feels good and it feels like you're making progress.

It's uncomfortable to take action, because you're stepping into the real world. I know, because I've wasted years waiting for things to be just right.

Eventually I discovered that conditions will never be perfect. That's when I just started. I started before I was ready because I was so sick of my own excuses.

Most people have to reach that point before they move forward. If you're not there yet, don't worry. One of the problems you'll bump into is self-criticism.

We are bombarded with advertising and ideas from friends, family, society and media. They tell us we have to do something or become someone to be okay. But you don't. You just have to be who you already are.

When you realize that you are already whole, complete and good enough, you'll start feeling better instantly.

Time to Write

This is probably the most important question in this book, because nothing matters unless you use what you've learned.

You have to be willing to move forward. If you haven't explored any other question in this book, then do yourself a favor and explore this one right now.

And start by exploring the first question, "How could I take the next step?"

Then dive into the prompts:
- The tiny, tiny next step I can take is …

- After going through this book, I feel like my next step is …

- If I were to listen to my heart, my tiny next step would be …

- The biggest insight I've gotten from reading this book is …

You see, you can't always see where the road may lead, which is why moving forward is essential. And with each step forward, you'll see opportunities you couldn't see before.

And that brings us to the end of the questions segment for this book, but I have a bonus surprise in store for you.

How to Solve Problems

We're coming to the end of this book. In question #16, you got tips from the future version of you, and in this section, I wanted to take the same concept further.

The goal is to have a conversation with yourself on paper or on your computer. I often do this when I'm feeling confused, and it helps.

The reason this works is because if you try to hold everything in your head, you can't think straight. You end up going in circles, and you get sidetracked. But when you write things down, you constantly see where you're at and it keeps you focused.

Example

To really show you how I do this, here's an example from my life of when my girlfriend and I packed our bags and moved to Spain for a year:

> *Henri #1: I'm feeling very anxious about this move to Spain.*
> *Henri #2: What specifically are you anxious about?*
> *Henri #1: I have no idea what's going to happen. We're moving to a new country. There's so much to do, and so much to think about.*
> *Henri #2: How is that a problem?*
> *Henri #1: It feels overwhelming.*
> *Henri #2: But can you do anything about it now?*
> *Henri #1: Not really. I guess that's how anxiety works.*

Henri #2: Yup. Anxiety often happens when you try to solve a future problem that you can't do anything about right now.

Henri #1: The solution then is to do what I can do now. I've prepared and I'll do my best when I get there.

Henri #2: Remember that any big move will be uncomfortable. It's hard-wired into us. We enjoy being comfortable.

Henri #1: Good point.

And there you have it, an example from inside my mind. Having a conversation like this helps you think straight.

Try it.

Possible Roadblocks

I've been coaching and helping people for the last few years, so I have a slight advantage in coaching myself. However, the more you do this, the better you get. Your next step is simply to start.

You don't have to do it in the same way I do. Just have a conversation with yourself, or just write your thoughts down on paper. There are no rules.

I don't really have a structure for how I do things. I just do whatever feels right. I'll repeat this once again: there is no right or wrong way to do this.

What matters is that you do it.

Time to Write

You'd be surprised by how resourceful you truly are. You can come up with solutions to your "problems" quite easily when you start coaching yourself.

The key is to constantly keep coming back to the present moment. Here are a few questions you can use:

1. What can I do now?
2. Is this relevant right now?
3. What is my next step?
4. How can I solve this?
5. How is this a problem?
6. What specifically is stopping me?
7. If I pretended to know, what would the solution be?

Keep going deeper and focus on asking questions that give you practical answers. If you don't come up with an answer, take a break, and let your brain do the work for you.

The Truth

Living a passionate life doesn't happen overnight. It's hard work, and it's not as glamorous as people make it out to be.

However, this doesn't mean you shouldn't go after it. It simply means that it takes more work than you'd expect.

But it's work worth doing, because once you gain momentum, your life will change. You will feel more fulfilled, excited, and happy.

You will start waking up in the morning being grateful for the life you're living.

Getting to this place means going through overwhelm, confusion and fear. Even now when I'm living a passionate life and doing work I love, I still experience fear.

It's a part of the game.

It's a part of being human.

You may not be crystal clear on what your passion is right now. That's okay. You simply have to get started.

And that is what this book has been all about.

I want you to take the next step, no matter how small it is, because when you do, things will start to unfold before your eyes.

And remember to take breaks and daydream. Let your brain chew on what you've learned here. Don't be in a rush to figure things out, because they'll figure themselves out in time.

Your Gift

In the beginning of this book, I promised you a free gift.

This free gift is a worksheet with each of the questions and their prompts in a PDF file. This will allow you to print it out and go through the questions one by one.

You can go through one question per day and it'll make it easy for you to see where you left off.

I've also added a few bonus questions at the end, because that's the way I roll. I like to surprise you with good stuff.

Now, you will have to sign-up to an email list to get this bonus. This is so I can stay in touch with you and get feedback. You can also interact with me through the list if you have questions or feedback.

I hate spam like anyone else, so I'm not going to abuse the privilege.

This worksheet is 100% free and exclusively available for the buyers of this book. You can get it at http://www.wakeupcloud.com/bookbonus

Next Step

You've just read, *Find Your Passion. 25 Questions You Must Ask Yourself*, where you learned to uncover what your passion and interests might be.

But do you know where to take things from here? It's not enough to find your passion, you also have to discover how to live a passionate life, which is why I wrote my next book: *Follow Your Heart: 21 Days to a Happier, More Fulfilling Life*.

This book will show you how I live a passionate life. You'll get practical tips that you can implement right away.

If you're interested in learning more, you can find my books at http://amazon.com/author/henri

If you're outside the U.S. go to your Amazon store and type in "Henri Junttila" and my books should pop up. If not, shoot me an email.

Thank You

We've come to the end of this book.

I just want to say thank you for reading. I truly appreciate it.

Seeing you succeed is what makes my heart sing. So if you have any questions or just want to share your insights with me, feel free to email me at henri@wakeupcloud.com. I see every email.

I'll do my best to answer your email. If you don't hear from me, the email has probably been hijacked by cyberspace pirates. If that happens, just email me again.

Connect

If you resonated with this book, you'll probably want to know where you can find me. I recommend you come over to my blog at http://www.wakeupcloud.com/.

If you want to connect via social media, you can find me on:

Facebook: http://www.facebook.com/WakeUpCloud
Twitter: http://www.twitter.com/henrijunttila
Shoot me a message and say hi.
Thanks in advance. You rock!
Now take action.

Made in United States
North Haven, CT
02 June 2022

19797420R00046